Oxford Progressive English Readers
*General Editor: D.H. Howe*

# The Golden Touch
# and Other Stories

The *Oxford Progressive English Readers* series provides a wide range of reading for learners of English. It includes classics, the favourite stories of young readers, and also modern fiction. The series has five grades: the *Introductory Grade* at a 1400 word level, *Grade 1* at a 2100 word level, *Grade 2* at a 3100 word level, *Grade 3* at a 3700 word level and *Grade 4* which consists of abridged stories. Structural as well as lexical controls are applied at each level.

Wherever possible the mood and style of the original stories have been retained. Where this requires departure from the grading scheme, glosses and notes are given.

All the books in the series are attractively illustrated. Each book also has a short section containing questions and suggested activities for students.

# The Golden Touch
# and Other Stories

Retold by Rosemary Border

Hong Kong
OXFORD UNIVERSITY PRESS
Oxford Singapore Tokyo
1984

*Oxford University Press*

*Oxford London New York Toronto*
*Kuala Lumpur Singapore Hong Kong Tokyo*
*Delhi Bombay Calcutta Madras Karachi*
*Nairobi Dar es Salaam Cape Town*
*Melbourne Auckland*

*and associated companies in*
*Beirut Berlin Ibadan Mexico City Nicosia*

© *Oxford University Press 1984*
*This edition first published 1984*

*OXFORD is a trade mark of Oxford University Press*

*Retold by Rosemary Border*
*Illustrated by Derek Collard*

*Simplified according to the language grading scheme*
*especially compiled by D.H. Howe*

*ISBN 0 19 581575 0*

*Printed in Hong Kong by Hip Shing Offset Printing Fty.*
*Published by Oxford University Press, Warwick House, Hong Kong*

# Contents

# Pronunciation Guide

———

| | |
|---|---|
| Arachnidae | /əˈræknɪdaɪ/ |
| Arachne | /əˈræknɪ/ |
| Minerva | /mɪnˈɜːvə/ |
| Midas | /ˈmaɪdæs/ |
| Dionysus | /ˌdaɪəˈnaɪsəs/ |
| Silenus | /saɪˈliːnəs/ |
| Apollo | /əˈpɒləʊ/ |
| Pan | /pæn/ |
| Theseus | /ˈθiːsjəs/ |
| Minotaur | /ˈmaɪnətɔː/ |
| Minos | /ˈmaɪnɒs/ |
| Daedalus | /ˈdiːdələs/ |
| Aegeus | /ˈiːdʒəs/ |
| Ariadne | /ˌærɪˈædnɪ/ |
| Icarus | /ˈɪkərəs/ |
| Perdix | /ˈpɜːdɪks/ |
| Pluto | /ˈpluːtəʊ/ |
| Proserpine | /ˈprɒsəpaɪn/ |
| Ceres | /ˈsɪəriːz/ |
| Olympus | /əˈlɪmpəs/ |
| Jupiter | /ˈdʒuːpɪtə/ |
| Orpheus | /ˈɔːfjəs/ |
| Eurydice | /jʊˈrɪdɪsɪ/ |

# 1
## The First Spider

===

Many people dislike spiders. Housewives do not like
spiders' webs* in their homes. Many people think
spiders are ugly and some people are even afraid of
them. There are millions of spiders on Earth. The
scientific name for them is Arachnidae. There is a       5
legend*, behind this name. The legend tells the
story of a clever but unwise girl called Arachne. She
annoyed the goddess* Minerva and received a terrible punishment.

Long ago, Roman artists and engineers prayed to       10
Minerva. She was the goddess of knowledge, art and
all kinds of skills. Her father was Jupiter. He was
the chief of the Roman gods. Minerva had no mother,
however, and she was not born in the usual way.
The legend says that Minerva leapt out of the brain       15
of Jupiter with a sword in her hand. She was a fierce
goddess as well as a clever one and if anyone annoyed
her she could be very cruel.


*Arachne's skill*

In a little house in Greece a poor farmer and his
wife had a little daughter. The child's name was       20
Arachne. When she was still quite small she began

* *webs*, the threads which a spider makes; they look like a net.
* *legend*, an old story which has been told by parents to children for
  hundreds of years; the story sometimes has a hidden truth.
* *goddess*, a woman god.

1

to show great skill with thread and cloth of all kinds. Soon she became quite famous. Her skill made the whole family quite rich. She was able to sell her work for high prices.

By the time Arachne was grown up, people were travelling long distances to see her work. She was indeed wonderfully clever. She could take a pile of wool or cotton and spin* it into the softest, strongest, thinnest thread in the world. She could weave* the thread into a web of beautiful cloth. She could cover it with wonderful pictures in coloured thread. Her busy needle shot in and out of her web like a flash of lightning. Flowers and fruit, birds and clouds appeared there like magic.

'How wonderful!' everyone cried. 'What skill! What art!'

Rich and important people praised Arachne. They offered her large amounts of money for her pictures. At first she felt uncomfortable when they praised her. In her heart she was still just an ordinary girl from a poor, simple family. She hid her hot, red face in her hands and looked down at her feet.

Later, however, Arachne became quite used to praise and money. She bought her parents a nice house and she began to feel very pleased with herself.

## Minerva is angry

'I must be special after all,' Arachne said to herself. She became rather proud, and she often

*spin*, make wool, cotton or silk into a thread. *weave*, make threads into cloth.

boasted* about her skill to all her visitors.

One day a rich merchant travelled hundreds of miles to meet her. He offered her a very high price for a special piece of work. He wanted her to make a picture for his wife. Arachne spun the thread, and coloured it with leaves and fruit. She wove a wonderful web of purple and pink and gold. She added flowers and fruit. They were so real and life-like, the merchant wanted to reach out and touch them.

'This is unbelievable!' he cried. He handled the soft web and touched the fresh flowers. 'I have never seen anything like it. You spin and weave like a goddess. Only Minerva herself could do better.'

'Who says she could do better?' said Arachne with a proud little shake of her head. 'This is *my* best work, sir. No one, no one can spin or weave better than I can. I hear that the goddess Minerva spins and weaves a little in her free time. I have never seen the results of her work, however. Perhaps it *is* better than mine. I am ready to believe it but she will have to prove* it first!'

The goddess heard Arachne's proud words. She was hurt and angry.

'Who does this proud human think she is?' Minerva said to herself. 'I must pay her a visit. Perhaps there is some mistake. Perhaps she boasted a little in the heat of the moment*. If she is sorry about it, I will excuse her.'

The goddess took off her beautiful dress of purple and gold. She wrapped herself in an old grey

*boasted*, praised herself. *prove*, show that something is really true.
*in the heat of the moment*, a time when one is too excited to think about what one is saying.

3

blanket. She covered her beautiful hair with a black cloth. She leaned heavily on a stick. Then, by magic, she changed herself into an old woman with grey hair and black, broken teeth. She looked in her silver mirror. 'Very satisfactory,' she said. 'No one can possibly know me like this.'

*Arachne receives a visitor*

There was a knock at the door of Arachne's house. 'Come in!' she called. She was quite used to visitors. Already a circle of interested people stood around her seat. They were watching Arachne at work.

'Sit down,' said Arachne to the grey, bent old woman. 'I am spinning wool at the moment.' She had a pile of sheep's wool at her feet. Her busy fingers were spinning the wool into beautiful strong thread. Her hands moved so fast that Minerva could hardly see them.

'When I finish spinning this wool,' said Arachne after a few moments, 'I shall start weaving a new picture. Watch carefully. You do not often have a chance to see a real artist at work. They say the goddess Minerva herself is jealous of my skill.'

She started the web of her new picture. Trees and hills grew like magic before the eyes of her audience. As she worked, Arachne boasted. Minerva grew angrier and angrier.


## Advice from an old woman

Minerva stepped forward and laid a gentle hand on the girl's shoulder.

'Dear child,' she said, 'it is dangerous to boast too loudly about your skill. The gods may hear.'

'I want them to hear!' cried the proud, foolish girl. 'I want them to see for themselves! And if they are jealous, that will *prove* I'm better than they are!'

'Listen to an old woman's advice, dear. I have lived a long time, and I have met many clever, proud young people. Their lives did not always end happily. You spin and weave wonderfully well, but you are only human. Do not compare yourself with the gods. Ask Minerva's pardon for your foolish boasting. I promise you that she will forgive you.'

'Why should Minerva forgive me?' cried Arachne.

6

'I only spoke the truth, after all! You are only a poor old woman, and your mind is as weak as your poor tired body. I tell you, Minerva can come here and try her skill. I will *prove* that I spoke the truth. She must be afraid of the test. Why hasn't she come before?'

Then Minerva dropped her stick and stood up very straight. She tore the black cloth off her hair and she said a magic word. Arachne and her audience saw the tall goddess standing there in all her strength and beauty. The other people at once fell on their knees and prayed to Minerva. Only Arachne remained standing. She held her head up high and showed no sign of fear.

'So you are here after all!' she said. 'Let us start the test at once.'

## The test

Without another word the goddess and the girl began to work. The group at the back of the room watched. No one spoke; they were almost afraid to breathe.

In the centre of Minerva's web a picture began to grow. It told the story of foolish humans who disobeyed the gods. This story was meant for Arachne, but it did not worry her at all. She worked and worked. Her cheeks were pink and she breathed rather fast. Her fingers flew over the web. The beauty of her picture filled the audience with wonder and joy.

You could almost hear the waves on the sea-shore. You could almost feel the wind in the trees. You could almost reach out and touch the flowers.

When the people saw the subject of Arachne's picture, they were afraid. Arachne was telling a story. That story showed that even the gods can
5  sometimes make mistakes.

At last both pictures were finished. Now the gods never told lies, and Minerva had to tell the truth about Arachne's work. She had to admit that the girl had won. Arachne's skill was greater than her
10  own.

'You win,' Minerva said, but her face was like thunder. It hurt her to say it, and she wanted to punish Arachne for that. Arachne saw the angry look on the goddess's face. Suddenly she realized
15  how foolish she had been. She also realized that she was in terrible danger. She wanted to beg Minerva's pardon.

'Forgive me,' she said. But it was too late.

With a scream of anger and hate Minerva picked
20  up Arachne's beautiful web. She tore it into tiny pieces. She threw the pieces into the crowd. Then she picked up her stick and struck Arachne three times on the head.

Arachne was too proud to accept this. She wanted
25  to end her shame and unhappiness at once. She could not live after this terrible moment. She picked up a rope that was lying near her chair. She wanted to hang herself and end her unhappy life.

Minerva held her back. 'No, I won't let you die,
30  you wicked girl! From this moment, you shall hang from a thread. You shall spin and weave all your life. You shall bear the same punishment for ever and ever.'

In a moment all Arachne's pretty hair fell off

her head. Her face became very small, with great, shining black eyes. Her body became very small and black. Her beautiful busy fingers changed into long hairy legs. She was a spider, hanging on a thin silk thread from a corner of the ceiling. The people *5* watched as the busy little animal began to weave a web across the corner of the room. The thread was very thin and strong. The web was very beautiful. The first spider was getting ready to catch flies for her supper. *10*

Ever since then, the spider has spun its silk thread and woven its beautiful web. Even the scientific name, Arachnidae, reminds us of the foolish girl and the jealous goddess.

# 2
## The Golden Touch

———

Some people are very lucky. 'He has the Midas touch,' we say about these people. 'Everything he touches turns to gold.' By that, we mean, every-thing he does is successful. We do not mean that
5 everything *really* turns to gold.

Long ago, that is what happened to a king. He prayed for the golden touch. The gods granted* his wish, but it did not make him happy.

That king was Midas. He had everything — a
10 beautiful palace, with wonderful rose gardens, plenty of money and a loving family. He had whole rooms full of gold and silver but he always wanted more. Gold was the most important thing in his life. When he prayed to the gods, he did not pray for love, or
15 happiness, or goodness. He just hoped, wished and prayed for more gold. In the daytime he thought about it and at night he dreamt about it.

*An unexpected visitor*

Dionysus was the god of wine. He was a great drinker. His favourite drinking companion was
20 Silenus. Silenus was a satyr*. From his waist to his head he looked like a man but under his long hair were hairy ears like a goat's ears. From his waist to his feet he was a goat. He had hairy legs and a tail

*granted*, gave something which had been asked for. *satyr*, a kind of god with feet like a goat.

and sharp little hoofs*. He was Dionysus's greatest friend, and the god was very fond of him.

One morning King Midas went for a walk in his rose garden. There he found Silenus asleep. He was lying under a rose-bush. There were several empty wine bottles beside him and there was a happy smile on his foolish face. Midas shouted to his servants. They at once made Silenus a prisoner but he did not mind much. He just lay down in his new bed and fell asleep again. Midas ordered his men to be kind to him. He was a greedy king, but he was not cruel.

Dionysus looked everywhere for his friend. At last he found where Silenus was, and came to see Midas. He begged the king to let his friend go.

'He did not mean to come into your garden,' said Dionysus. 'Please let me take him home. If you do, I will grant you a wish.'

'*Any* wish?' said Midas. He licked his lips. 'What shall I wish for?' he said to himself. He thought about piles of gold, whole palaces made of gold, ships full of gold. What should he wish for? Suddenly he had an idea. 'I wish,' he said aloud, 'for everything that I touch to turn to gold.'

### The wish is granted

Dionysus looked hard at the greedy king. 'Are you quite sure?' he asked. 'You want everything you touch to turn to gold?'

'That's right,' said Midas. 'Take your friend. He is awake now, and he has a terrible headache. Now

---

* *hoofs*, the feet of a horse, cow or goat.

grant me my wish! Let everything I touch turn to gold.'

'Your wish is granted already,' said the god. He gave a small, secret smile. 'And if you change your mind, just call for me.'

'I shall not change my mind!' said Midas. 'Thank you, Dionysus, for granting my wish. You have made me the happiest man in the world!'

As soon as the visitors had gone, Midas tested his new skill. He touched the heavy wooden table. It became cold, hard metal. It shone like the sun.

'Gold!' cried Midas. 'It works!' Laughing like a naughty little boy, he touched all the walls of the room. They turned to gold too. 'Whee!' shouted the king. 'I'm the richest man in the world!' He touched the curtains at the windows. At once they hung in stiff gold folds.

Midas sang and shouted. A small insect flew in through the window. It landed on Midas's nose. At once it fell down dead on the floor. Midas picked it up and examined it. The insect was all gold, from the top of its tiny head to the tips of its wings. It looked like a very lovely and perfect piece of jewellery.

'Now I do not need to buy gold jewellery for my wife. I can make it myself! I will make gold presents for my little daughter too,' Midas said.

Midas spent hours practising his new skill. He changed everything in the room into gold. Then he went out into his rose garden. He found Silenus's empty bottles. He changed those into gold. Then he started on the garden itself. Soon it was full of stiff, dead gold flowers, trees and grass. He could not touch the birds. They were too quick for him. They

12

flew among the golden trees looking very puzzled.

Midas picked a big bunch of gold roses. He took them into the palace and put them in a vase. The vase changed to gold as soon as he touched it.

'I am the richest man in the whole world,' said *5* Midas to himself. 'I have the golden touch. Thank you, great Dionysus, for granting my wish.'

## The gold statue*

Just then there was a knock at the door. 'Come in!' called the king. The door opened and his little daughter entered. She was a sweet, pretty child and *10* the king loved her very much.

'How strange everything looks, Father,' the child said. She looked in surprise at the gold room. She picked up the tiny gold insect from the table.

'What a pretty little thing,' she said. 'It is just like *15* a real insect.'

'It is better than a real insect, dear,' said her father. 'It is made of gold.'

'I like your roses, Father,' the girl said. She touched the gold roses in their gold vase. 'They look *20* just like real ones.' She held a stiff gold rose near her nose. 'What a pity they have no smell.'

King Midas watched her. To him she seemed the loveliest thing in his whole kingdom. Without thinking, he reached out and touched her hand. *25*

At once the warmth left her body. She was cold and stiff. King Midas was holding a beautiful gold statue.

---

* *statue*, a shape made from wood or stone that looks like a person or animal.

'What have I done?' he cried. He shouted for his servants. They were puzzled and unhappy. The King was too hurt and sad to explain. The servants carried the beautiful gold statue upstairs. They laid it on the
5 bed. Midas's queen hurried forward to comfort him.

He stepped back with a cry. 'Don't touch me!' he screamed. 'Can't you see? Everything I touch turns to gold. Look what happened to our child! Keep away!' He ran upstairs and lay down on his bed.

*Hunger and thirst*

10 He could not sleep that night. As soon as he laid his head on the pillow it became hard and cold. There was no warmth in his stiff gold blankets. He was lonely without his wife. He was afraid to lie next to her, of course. He did not want to find
15 another gold statue beside him in the morning.

When he got up he was very hungry and thirsty. He could not eat or drink, however. Every bite of food turned to gold in his mouth. He tried to drink some water. Every drop turned to gold. He had to
20 spit it out.

'I shall die of hunger and thirst!' he said. He realized his danger now. He was going to die like a beggar with all his gold around him.

'What can I do?' he cried.

25 The queen was a gentle, wise woman. 'Ask Dionysus to help you,' she said. 'He granted your wish, after all. He must be able to take it away again.'

Midas realized she was right. He went out into the
30 still golden rose garden and began to pray. At once

16

Dionysus appeared before him. The god was smiling.

'Well,' said Dionysus, looking around, 'I see you have been busy. Has your golden touch made you happy?'

Midas fell on his knees. 'It has brought me unhappiness,' he said. He told the story of his little daughter. 'I miss her terribly,' he said. 'And I have just realized that I am going to die of hunger and thirst too. Please, please take back the golden touch. I don't want it any more. I want to hold my little daughter in my arms again. I want to kiss my dear wife. I want to eat and drink again. Please, Dionysus, forgive me, and make me ordinary again!'

## *Midas's wish is granted*

'Very well,' said Dionysus. 'I will grant your wish once more. Go to the river and bathe in the water. Then everything will be all right again.'

King Midas ran down to the river and threw himself in. When he came out again he touched the grass of the river bank. Was it going to turn to gold? No. It remained green and soft. He hurried back to his palace. His little daughter ran to greet him. He held her in his arms.

'Oh, Father,' she said, 'I've had such a strange dream! I dreamed I was a statue. Wasn't that silly?'

Midas looked round his palace. The golden walls, floor and furniture were no longer there. A small insect sat on a curtain. It was cleaning its wings. 'Is it the same insect?' Midas asked himself. 'I shall never know.' He looked out of the window at his gardens. The flowers danced in the sunshine.

Servants brought dishes of food and jugs of wine, and Midas ate and drank. To him the simple meal seemed like a feast. He held his queen's hand while his little daughter sat on his knee. 'I will never be greedy again,' he said to himself.

This is only a legend. All the same, there is something strange about the river in Midas's kingdom. Its sand is very rich in gold. If you wash it, you will find gold-dust.

# 3
## The Donkey's Ears

———

'A secret is too little for one, enough for two, too much for three.' There is a lot of truth in that saying.

Apollo was the god of music and art. Everyone agreed that Apollo's music was the most beautiful of all, that is everyone except one foolish king. Here *5* is the legend of that king, and the story of Apollo's punishment.

Another of the gods was fond of music too. His name was Pan. He was the god of the woods and rivers, sheep and cattle. Pan looked like a very *10* beautiful human boy, until you saw his ears and legs. He had hairy ears like a goat's. He had goat's legs too, and little sharp hoofs.

Pan picked some of the reeds* that grew by the river. He made some pipes from the reeds, and he *15* played music on them. The satyrs and nymphs* came to listen. Nymphs were unimportant goddesses who did not live on Olympus with the chief gods. They lived with the satyrs near the woods, hills and streams. They liked Pan's wild, sweet music very *20* much.

### Midas hears the music

The music reached human ears too. King Midas was in his rose garden one morning when he heard

*reeds*, tall, thin plants that grow beside rivers. *nymphs*, kinds of goddesses who live in the woods and streams.

19

the sound of Pan's reed pipes. The sweet music pleased him very much. He left his garden and joined the audience of nymphs and satyrs on the river bank. He clapped loudly and shouted for more.

5 After that the king often listened to Pan's music. He praised it loudly. 'I think it is the best music of all,' the king said. 'Even better than Apollo's.'

This pleased the nymphs and satyrs. Pan was *their* god; they did not often see Apollo or hear his
10 music. 'Oh yes,' they all agreed. 'Much better than Apollo's.'

Pan enjoyed all the praise and clapping. He became very proud. 'I *am* greater than Apollo,' he said, 'but we must prove it, my friends. We must
15 have a contest*!'

When Apollo heard, he did not know whether to laugh or cry. 'Is this a joke?' he said to himself. 'Pan has always enjoyed a little fun. He can't be serious now — or *can* he? Well, I don't mind joining in his
20 little game.'

*The contest*

The nymphs and satyrs chose the place for the contest. It was the smooth, green side of a hill quite near Midas's palace. They asked the god of the hill to judge the contest. He was a dear old god with
25 long white hair and a sweet, kind face. They asked Midas to sit beside the judge. Midas was very proud and felt most important. A large audience of nymphs and satyrs gathered on the soft, green grass. They were all eager to begin the contest.

*contest, a game to decide who is the best at something.

20

The god Apollo stood in front of the judge. He held his shining gold lyre* in his hand. Pan stood beside him on his sharp little hoofs. He held his reed pipes. He saw Midas and smiled and waved to him.

At a sign from the judge the contest began. Pan  *5* played first. He lifted his reed pipes to his lips and blew. His music seemed to belong to the woods and rivers. The audience could almost hear the sound of the streams and the wind in the trees. It was wild, sweet, lonely music. It made the audience feel  *10* strange and uncomfortable. They wanted to go home to their forests and their rocky hillsides.

Midas clapped and cheered loudly, but the nymphs and satyrs were strangely silent.

Now it was Apollo's turn to play. He touched the  *15* golden strings of his lyre. He played and sang for a long time. The nymphs and satyrs sat as still as statues.

Apollo's voice and lyre made a different kind of music. The sound seemed to reach out and touch  *20* everyone's heart. There were tears in the nymphs' eyes. The satyrs were unusually quiet and thoughtful. Only Midas looked a little bored.

## The winner

At last Apollo finished his song and the whole audience rose. They clapped until their hands ached.  *25* They cheered until their throats were sore. All except Midas. He gave a few polite little claps, then he turned to the judge of the contest.

*lyre, a musical instrument with strings which are played with the fingers.

'Very nice,' he said, 'but I still like Pan's music best.'

No one else agreed with the king. The judge gave Apollo the prize and the nymphs and satyrs crowded
5  round him. Pan stood alone under a tree. He looked rather hurt and angry.

'I *still* like Pan's music best,' said Midas loudly. He turned to go back to his palace.

Apollo heard the king's words. 'Do you?' he said
10  softly. He looked hard at Midas.

'Yes, I do,' said Midas. 'Now excuse me; I must go.'

'There must be something wrong with your ears, King Midas,' said Apollo. He reached out and
15  touched the king's head. 'Goodbye, King Midas,' he said. 'Remember me.'


*The donkey's ears*

Next morning Midas woke up and began to comb his hair. There was something big and soft on the left-hand side of his head. He felt it. It was covered
20  with hair. He felt the other side of his head. There was something there too. He ran to the mirror. Instead of his own small, pink ears he had the grey, hairy ears of a donkey.

'Someone has played a joke on me,' he said to
25  himself. 'A good joke too! I'll just pull these silly ears off, then I'll have a good laugh.'

He pulled at the soft grey ears but cried out in pain. The ears were part of him; it was not a joke!

Suddenly Midas remembered Apollo's touch the
30  day before. He remembered the god's words. 'There

22

must be something wrong with your ears.'

What a punishment! What could he do?

'I mustn't let anyone know,' said Midas. He looked in a cupboard and found a long piece of red cloth.
5 Carefully he bent the long ears over the top of his head. He tied the cloth round his head and fastened it with a gold pin. He looked rather strange, but there was no sign of his ears. Under the cloth they felt hot and uncomfortable, but his secret was safe.

## Midas's secret

10 At breakfast everyone looked at the king's strange hat. No one said anything, however. In those days kings could do exactly as they liked. No one ever questioned them. The queen gave him a puzzled look when they were alone together. Midas said
15 nothing. He did not care what she thought. He did not want her to know the truth.

For a long time Midas kept his secret. He slept with his head covered. He ate with his head covered. He even bathed with his head covered. Many men
20 did the same. It became smart to wear a hat all the time.

Sometimes Midas wore a tall gold hat. That was the most comfortable, because his ears could stand up straight. Sometimes he folded them under a cap.
25 In the bath he covered them with a towel. No one — not even the queen — saw the king without anything on his head.

'Perhaps he has lost his hair,' the servants whispered. 'He is ashamed to let anyone see.' Midas
30 heard, but he did not care. His secret was still safe.

## Midas calls the barber*

At last, however, Midas's hair under his hats became very long and uncomfortable. 'I must have a haircut,' he said to himself, 'but I can't cut my own hair. If someone does it for me, he will discover my secret!'  *5*

Midas called his barber. 'I need a haircut,' he said. 'Please start at once. If anything surprises you, say nothing. If you keep my secret I will reward you well. If you tell anyone you will die a terrible death.'

The barber was very puzzled, but he agreed to cut  *10* Midas's hair. 'I promise I won't tell anyone,' he said. 'Now let me cut your hair.'

Midas took off his cap. The big grey ears sprang up on either side of his head. The barber wanted to laugh aloud, but he was too afraid of the king. He  *15* changed his laugh into a little cough, and started work.

When he had finished, he accepted the king's money. He promised once more to keep the king's secret. He folded the silly ears over the top of the  *20* king's head and put the cap over them.

'Remember,' said Midas. 'Don't tell anyone.'

'Your secret is safe with me, great King,' said the barber.

The barber tried very hard to keep his secret. He  *25* never said a word to anyone but in his mind's eye he could see those foolish ears and the king's weak, silly face between them. He wished he could share the joke with his family. Sometimes he thought about the donkey's ears, and laughed aloud.  *30*

*barber*, someone whose job it is to cut people's hair.

25

'What's the matter?' his wife asked many times.

'Nothing, dear,' said the barber. At night he dreamed of those grey ears. He wanted to tell his wife about his dreams, but he feared the king's anger.

### King Midas has donkey's ears

5   At last the barber could bear it no longer. He went down to the river bank and dug a hole in the ground. Then he bent down and put his mouth near the hole and very softly he whispered into the earth, 'King Midas has donkey's ears.'

10   At once he felt better. 'I've kept my promise,' he said. 'I haven't told anyone.'

He filled the hole with earth again and went home.

Spring came to Midas's kingdom. New leaves grew on the trees and fresh young reeds grew by the 15 river. The wind blew through the reeds. 'Sh — sh,' said the reeds. All except one little group of reeds near King Midas's palace. They whispered, 'King Midas has donkey's ears! King Midas has donkey's ears!'

20   A fisherman was sitting on the bank hoping to catch a fish. He heard the whispering reeds. He hurried home and told his family. Soon the whole kingdom knew the king's secret. The barber escaped to another country but the king really could not 25 blame the barber. He never told the secret to anyone, did he?

# 4
## Theseus and the Minotaur*

Not far from Greece is the island of Crete. A king of
the island was called Minos, and he had a very
strange pet. It was called the Minotaur, after its
master. The bottom half of its body was human. The
rest of it, however, was like a great black bull*.      5
Minos's clever servant Daedalus (there is more
about him in the next story) built a home for the
Minotaur. This place was called the labyrinth*.
It was under the ground. Hundreds of twisting,
turning paths led to an open space in the centre      10
where the terrible Minotaur lived. Its favourite food
was human meat, and Minos fed it every day on
criminals and prisoners. He just left them at the
entrance to the labyrinth. He knew no one could
possibly find the way out. Sooner or later they      15
reached the centre, and the Minotaur had a feast.

### Aegeus and Theseus

Meanwhile, in Athens, King Aegeus ruled the city
and the land around it. Now, when Aegeus was still
a young prince he spent some time in a small quiet
village. There he met a pretty girl and fell in love      20
with her. They had a baby boy and named him
Theseus. But when Theseus was only a few months

*Minotaur, an animal, half man and half bull. *bull, a male cow.
*labyrinth, a place under the ground with many twisting and turning
paths which lead to an open space in the centre.

27

old, Aegeus's father died. He had to return to Athens to rule the kingdom. He left his little son behind. Before he left, however, he buried his sword in the ground and covered the place with a heavy,
5   flat stone.

'My dear,' he said to Theseus's mother, 'when our son is big and strong, take him to this place. Let him lift the stone and take my sword. It is his, as soon as he can get it for himself. Then he must go to Athens
10  and see me and I shall make him my heir*.'

He kissed her goodbye and started on the long road to Athens.

At about the same time that Theseus was born, King Minos also became the father of a baby boy.
15  Minos loved his child very much and took great care of him. The prince grew tall, strong and intelligent. Everyone was fond of him.

### The festival at Athens

Every year the people of Athens had a festival. All the young men of Greece and the islands near by
20  met there. They took part in all kinds of games and contests. Everyone wanted to join in the feasting and fun. Minos's son begged his father to let him travel to Athens too. Minos was not sure.

'You are my son and my heir,' he told the young
25  prince. 'What if something happens to you? What will I do then?'

'Oh, Father, nothing can happen to me!' cried the prince of Crete. 'I just want to go to the festival like

---

* *heir*, the person who will have one's money, kingdom etc. after one's death.

all the other boys. Please say, yes, Father! Please!'

With a heavy heart Minos agreed. He and his little daughter, Ariadne, waved goodbye and wished him good luck.

Before long everyone in Athens knew and liked the prince of Crete. He did very well in all the contests, but he never boasted about his skill. Everyone, except King Aegeus, was very fond of him. The king was very jealous of the young stranger.

One night, when the prince was on his way back to Crete, King Aegeus sent some men after him. They murdered him and hid his body in the woods. Minos waited on the harbour wall for his son's ship. It returned without him.

The people of Athens were sad too. They did not know what had happened to the young prince. They only knew that he was lost. Only King Aegeus knew the truth.

A few days after this, Aegeus's own son appeared in Athens.

For Theseus this was the happy end of a long and difficult journey. It all began on the day when he lifted the heavy stone. He took the sword from under it. Then he kissed his mother goodbye. He had many adventures on the long road to Athens. There were wild animals, robbers and murderers.

## Theseus arrives

Theseus defeated them all. He arrived in Athens and Aegeus knew him at once. 'My heir has come! We must have a feast!' the king shouted. He opened the gates of his palace to all the people. There was

29

feasting and fun for several days. Wine poured from the palace fountains and there was free food for everyone. The people of Athens forgot the prince of Crete and greeted their own young prince.

5     Meanwhile Minos was still waiting for his son. At last some travellers found the boy lying dead in the woods. They sent messengers to Minos. The king sent for his son's body and ordered a great funeral. He was very angry.

10     'Those Greeks killed my son,' he said to himself. 'They will pay for this!' He gathered a large army and sailed across the sea to Athens. Minos was going to attack the city.

## Surrender*!

    Minos reached Athens with his army. They
15 marched to the city. Of course, the gates were closed and the walls were well guarded. Aegeus was expecting them.

    This did not worry Minos, however. He and his men had plenty of food. They also had plenty of
20 time so they made their camp outside the city walls. They put up their comfortable tents and began to cook their supper. 'All we have to do,' said King Minos to his captains, 'is wait patiently. Soon Athens will be ours.'

25     The captains knew the king was right. Athens depended on the farms outside the city for food. Minos and his men stopped the carts from entering Athens. No one could go into the city. No one could

*surrender, admit someone else has won the battle.

30

leave it without becoming a prisoner. In a week or two everyone in Athens was hungry. Soon children and old people became weak and ill. A few people died.

'They will surrender soon,' Minos told his men.      *5*

They saw their leader's cold, hard face. 'His son's death has changed him,' they whispered to each other. 'He has no pity.'

It hurt Aegeus to see his people so weak and ill. 'We must surrender,' he said at last to his wise men.      *10*
'I cannot bear to let this continue.' He sent a messenger to the king of Crete. In his message Aegeus offered to surrender. He asked Minos to show pity to his poor people.

Minos read the message, and he laughed. It was a      *15*
cold, cruel laugh. 'Pity!' he said. 'What pity did the people of Athens show towards my son?'

The messenger came back to Athens with a white face and shaking hands. 'Great King,' he said to Aegeus, 'King Minos will leave our city if you      *20*
promise something.'

'I'll promise anything! Anything!' cried Aegeus.

## Food for the Minotaur

'Every year you must send seven young men and seven girls to Crete. There, Minos will give them to the Minotaur.'      *25*

King Aegeus gave a great cry. 'How can I allow this?' he cried.

The wise men of the city said, 'Do you want *all* your people to die of hunger, Great King? If you agree to Minos's conditions, only a few will die.'      *30*

31

With a heavy heart King Aegeus agreed to Minos's conditions. The people of Athens chose their young people. It was a sad business. The wise men put small black and white balls into an iron pot.
5　Each boy took a ball out of the pot. If it was white, he was safe but only for one year. There were seven black balls. If a boy took a black ball, then he was one of the unlucky seven. The families watched in hope and fear.

10　Then it was the girls' turn to crowd around the pot. Seven black balls; seven crying mothers. The fourteen unlucky people went away with King Minos to their death.

The next year the same terrible thing happened.
15　The people of Athens were very unhappy and ashamed, but they were afraid of King Minos. They could not break their promise. The next year after that, however, Prince Theseus stepped forward.

### Theseus goes to Crete

'Give me a black ball!' he shouted to the wise men.
20　'I am not going to let my friends go to their death without me. I want to kill the Minotaur and make our country free. If I fail, I shall be proud to die with my friends.'

'Don't go, Theseus!' begged the king. 'You are my
25　son and my heir. Don't leave your poor old father alone!'

'What about all the other parents?' said Theseus. 'No, Father, this cannot continue. I have to do something about it. If I don't, all the parents in Athens
30　will live in fear. I must try to kill the Minotaur.'

A ship with black sails waited in the harbour. King Aegeus stood with the other parents on the harbour wall and waved goodbye. In his heart he was sorry for his cruel murder. Now he understood how King Minos felt. He cried tears of shame. 5

Theseus saw his father crying. 'Don't be sad!' he called. 'I *shall* kill the Minotaur. Watch for this ship. I shall take down the black sails, and put up white ones. When you see the white sails, you will know I am safe and well.' 10

'I shall watch every day,' cried Aegeus. 'Goodbye, my dear son and good luck!'

## Ariadne

Theseus was cheerful all through the sad journey to Crete. The others almost believed him. They reached the island and were taken to see King 15 Minos. The king saw their white, frightened faces. For a moment he was sorry for them, and he was sorry for their parents too. Then he saw in his mind's eye the body of his own murdered boy. All pity left his heart. 20

His daughter Ariadne stood beside him. She was a beautiful girl with a kind, gentle heart. She saw the boys and girls and she thought of the dark labyrinth. She thought of the cruel Minotaur and tears filled her eyes. 25

King Minos saw Theseus and his eyes shone. 'Surely this is the young prince of Athens!' he said.

Theseus stepped forward. 'I am Theseus, son of Aegeus,' he said. 'Great King, please let my companions sleep in peace in the palace yard tonight. They 30 are tired after the journey. Let me enter the labyrinth alone. The others can follow me in the morning.'

'So the prince is proud!' said Minos. 'He wishes to
5 die alone. Very well, Prince Theseus, I will grant your wish.'

Meanwhile Ariadne was looking at the brave young prince. Her cheeks were pink and her heart was beating like a drum. Her eyes shone with love
10 and pity. 'I *won't* let him die!' she said to herself. 'There must be a way to save him.'

'Father,' she said aloud, 'let me lead the prince to the labyrinth tonight. He is a king's son, and I am a king's daughter. I am the right person to do it.'

## To the labyrinth

15 King Minos agreed. When it was dark Ariadne led Theseus to the entrance of the labyrinth. It was a clear night. The silver moon shone and a light wind blew the black sails of Theseus's ship. They reached the gate of the labyrinth.

20 'Prince Theseus,' said Ariadne, 'my heart is heavy for you. You are brave and strong, and your sword is sharp. Why can't you kill the Minotaur tonight, and escape with your companions? As soon as the Minotaur is dead your promise to my father will
25 mean nothing. Athens will be safe and *you* —' She stopped, and looked down at the ground.

Theseus gave her a warm, grateful smile. 'Lady,' he said, 'my arm is strong. I hope I shall kill the Minotaur. Then my companions will be able to
30 escape. But I shall have to stay behind. You see, I

34

shall never find my way out of the labyrinth. Everyone says it is impossible.'

'It is not impossible,' whispered Ariadne. She gave him a ball of thin, strong thread. 'Fasten one end of this to the gate. Hold the ball tight in your left *5* hand. When you have killed the Minotaur, you must follow the thread. Roll it up as you go along. It may save your life!'

'Thank you a thousand times!' breathed Theseus. He kissed her and touched her hand. He tasted the *10* salt tears on her cheeks. Then he tied the thread to the gate and entered the labyrinth.

## *Saved by a thread*

He followed the strange, twisted path that led to the Minotaur. It was dark and quiet. Theseus could smell the Minotaur's hot breath. The smell grew *15* stronger. Then he heard heavy breathing.

A black shape lay in front of him. It was darker than the darkness around him. The great black sides of the Minotaur moved like the sea with the beating of its great black heart. It was asleep. It *20* was not expecting food. *That* usually arrived in the morning. It was dreaming of soft, sweet young girls.

Very quietly Theseus crept up to the Minotaur. With one blow of his sword he cut off its head. The *25* hot black blood poured out and boiled on the ground at Theseus's feet. He stepped back quickly. Then he felt for the thread in the darkness, and followed it.

He followed that thread through every dark twist and turn of the mysterious labyrinth. He rolled it *30*

35

up, and the ball of thread grew bigger. The journey seemed to last for ever. Surely something was wrong. Surely he was lost in the dark. Every bone in his body ached. His heart beat inside his chest like a frightened bird. 'I'll never get out of here,' he thought. He continued to wind the thread.

5

36

At last he saw the moon. He had reached the
entrance. The end of the thread was still tied to the
gate.

And there stood Ariadne! She had a basket of
food and a leather bottle of water. He ran to her and
took her in his arms. He kissed her and thanked her

5

37

again and again. Then he told her his story while he ate and drank.

## *Escape!*

'And now I must sleep,' he said at last.

'No, Prince Theseus!' said Ariadne. 'You must
5 escape now! Wake your companions and tell them the glad news. Then sail away before my father wakes. It is your only chance.'

'And leave you behind?' said Theseus. 'What will your father do to you? Do you think he will reward
10 you for your part in our escape? No, Ariadne, I'm taking you with me. You have saved my life, and I love you with all my heart. Come back to Athens and be my wife!'

'I fell in love with you the moment I saw you,'
15 breathed Ariadne. 'I will go with you but we must hurry! Wake your friends before it is too late!'

Theseus gathered the others together. They were still rubbing their eyes as he led them down to the harbour. They sang and shouted as they sailed back
20 to Athens.

They forgot one thing. They forgot to take down the black sails. They were all so happy, they never thought about King Aegeus on the harbour wall.

He stood and watched for his son's ship. At last
25 he saw a dark shape in the distance. It came nearer, and he saw the black sails. He thought his son had been killed by the Minotaur. With a cry he threw himself into the sea and drowned.

Ever since then, the sea near Athens has been
30 called the Aegean Sea, after him. Theseus became

king of Athens and Ariadne was his queen. Athens was free, and Theseus ruled over the city for many happy years.

# 5
## The Wonderful Wings

Long ago in the city of Athens there lived a man
named Daedalus. He was the cleverest artist in the
city. He made wonderful statues and he was also a
most skilful builder. All the rich men of Athens
5 asked Daedalus to build palaces for them. He filled
them with statues and fountains and other wonderful things.

Not far from Athens was the island of Crete.
Minos was King of Crete and he heard about
10 Daedalus's skill. He had a strange animal called the
Minotaur. This was a very dangerous pet, and
Minos needed a safe place for it. He asked Daedalus
for his advice.

As a result of this, Daedalus built the labyrinth.
15 There the Minotaur lived — until Theseus killed
it. You have already read that story. The labyrinth
was Daedalus's greatest piece of work. He was very
proud of it. Minos was very pleased with it and gave
Daedalus a large reward.
20 'Remember,' he told Daedalus, 'come here when-
ever you like. You will always be welcome here.'

Daedalus thanked the king and went back to his
workshop in Athens.


*Icarus and Perdix*

Daedalus's wife was dead. He looked after his
25 little son Icarus alone. Icarus was too young to help

40

his father in the workshop but he had an assistant. This was his nephew, Perdix. Perdix's parents were dead and his uncle took care of him. Perdix was a clever, eager boy. He wanted to be as skilful as his uncle. He listened carefully to every word Daedalus 5 said. He copied everything carefully. Daedalus was glad to have such an eager pupil. He taught Perdix everything he knew. He was a good teacher as well as a clever artist and builder. Soon the boy was making wonderful things. 10

Perdix was soon as skilful as his master. He used his skill in new and clever ways.

'One day,' the people of Athens said, 'Perdix will be a greater artist than his uncle.'

Daedalus was pleased and proud at first. Then he 15 began to feel hurt and jealous. He realized that his pupil was greater than he was. He could not bear that. All his love for his nephew turned to hate.

## The murder

One evening he invited Perdix to walk with him by the sea-shore. It was a beautiful calm summer 20 evening. The sun was going down into the dark blue sea. Daedalus led Perdix to the top of a high cliff*. Together they looked down at the water.

'The sea is a beautiful blue, Uncle,' said Perdix. 'I want to make curtains in exactly that colour. I shall 25 hang them in the temple of Athene. Don't you think they will look wonderful?'

He talked and talked about his work, and his

---

*cliff, a high place; a steep piece of rock at the edge of the sea.

41

plans for the future. He did not see the black anger in his uncle's eyes. Suddenly Daedalus stepped back a little. He gave the boy a hard push. Perdix found himself falling over the cliff edge. He tried to catch
5  hold of some grass, but it tore away in his hands. With a cry he fell down, down towards the rocks at the bottom of the cliff.

He did not die, however. The goddess Minerva heard his cry. She knew Perdix well and loved him
10  for his skill. She changed him into a small brown bird. He opened his wings and flew away over the sea.

### The escape to Crete

Daedalus realized he was in trouble. 'If anyone hears about this,' he said to himself, 'they will kill
15  me. I must escape at once.' He ran back to his workshop.

He packed a few things in an old bag. Then he woke his little son. 'Come on, Icarus,' he said, 'we must leave at once.'
20  'What's the matter?' asked Icarus. He was still sleepy. He rubbed his eyes and looked up into his father's worried face.

'We must leave Athens at once. If we don't, we shall be in terrible danger. Put your clothes on and
25  follow me quietly!'

They went down to the harbour. There they climbed into a little fishing boat. Icarus watched his father opening the sail. Daedalus was as good at sailing as he was at everything else.
30  'Where are we going, Father?' asked Icarus.

42

'To Crete, son. King Minos will make us welcome. He is my friend and will give me work but we must go quickly.'

## The prisoners

Minos remembered Daedalus's work on the labyrinth. He was glad to see him. He gave Daedalus a workshop and kept him very busy. Daedalus did some very good work for the king. 5

But one day Daedalus quarrelled with the king. It was not an important matter. Minos wanted something, and Daedalus spoke rudely to him. Minos was angry and Daedalus was too proud to ask the king's pardon. Big quarrels often start in small, unimportant ways. 10

'I'll teach *you* a lesson!' Minos shouted. 'Guards! Throw this man into prison. I will see him when he has learnt better manners.' 15

They locked Daedalus and little Icarus in a room at the top of a tall building. There Daedalus and his son lived for several weeks. Every day Icarus watched the birds that flew past his window. 20

'I wish we could fly like that, Father,' he said. 'Then we could fly away; we could be free!'

Daedalus said nothing. But already he had an idea. As the days went by that idea grew. He watched the seabirds and studied the way they flew. 25

One night Daedalus began to make some wings. He took feathers of different sizes. He stuck them with wax* to some thin pieces of wood. He used

---

* *wax*, something soft and yellow which bees make; it melts easily.

hundreds of feathers. At last the work was finished. There were two pairs of wings, a small pair and a large pair. The sun was just rising as Daedalus stood back and looked at his work.

### Flying away

5    'Wake up, Icarus!' he said. 'We are going to fly like the birds. Won't that be fun?'

Carefully he fastened the small pair of wings to Icarus's shoulders. Then he put on his own wings. He moved his arms up and down a few times. The
10 wings seemed to work very well. Would they carry his weight? He could not be sure.

'Follow me, son,' he said, 'and do exactly what I tell you. Don't fly too low. If you do, the water may wet your wings. Then you will fall into the sea and
15 drown. Do not fly too high either. I have stuck the feathers of your wings with wax. The heat of the sun will melt the wax. So take care!'

He kissed his little son. He climbed up to the window and stood there for a moment. Then he took
20 a deep breath and threw himself into space.

The air rushed past his face. For a moment he thought he was going to crash to the ground. Then he spread his arms out wide. The great wings opened. He was flying! He called out to Icarus.
25    'Jump, son, and spread out your arms. The wings will hold you up.'

Icarus closed his eyes and jumped. The wings opened wide. He was flying! It was a wonderful feeling. He joined his father. Together they looked
30 down at their prison. It looked very far away.

44

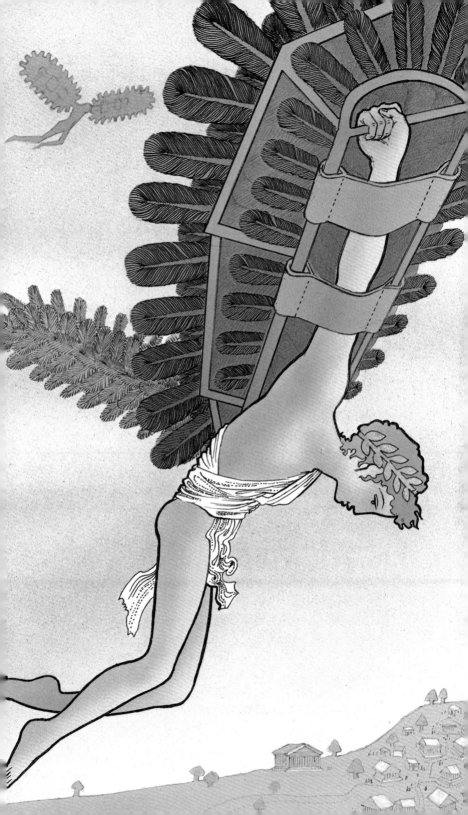

*Off to Sicily*

A guard was marching along the palace wall. He saw them and pointed up at them. To Daedalus and Icarus he looked like a toy soldier.

'Get your bows!' the captain of the guard shouted. 'Shoot them before they can get away!' The little toy soldiers ran about and shot at the two escaped prisoners. Daedalus just laughed. They were quite safe.

'Where are we going, Father?' asked Icarus.

'Sicily, I hope. I have friends there. We shall be safe.'

On and on they flew, over land and sea. Sailors watched them. 'Gods!' they cried. 'Quick! Down on your knees and pray!'

A fisherman thought they were two big birds. He tried to shoot them but they were too quick for him.

The sun rose higher in the sky. Icarus was becoming quite clever at flying. He practised diving down towards the sea. It was very exciting but he always remembered his father's words. He opened his wings before he came too near the water. He did not want to wet his wings.

Soon, however, he began to feel very brave and sure of himself. He saw birds flying far above him, above the clouds. He wanted to join them in the clear blue sky. He looked quickly towards his father. Daedalus was flying smoothly along. Every beat of his great wings was carrying him closer to Sicily.

Icarus saw his chance. He opened his wings wide and flew up, up towards the hot white sun. He was so happy, he forgot the wax on his feathers.

## *The heat of the sun*

The sun's fierce heat burned Icarus's face. Soon the wax around his feathers began to melt. One by one the feathers dropped from the wings. They fell like snow towards the sea. Icarus had nothing to hold him up. He was falling! In his fear he cried out to his father. *5*

Daedalus heard the boy's cries. He turned his head to look and he saw Icarus falling. He turned and flew towards the boy as fast as he could. Icarus hit the water and sank below the waves. His wings *10* floated on the water like two sad little boats.

Daedalus tore off his own wings and dived into the sea. He swam down until he found Icarus. He fought his way to the surface* with Icarus in his arms. He looked about for land. There was an island *15* in the distance. Daedalus swam on his back, holding Icarus under the arms. He prayed all the time. He made all kinds of promises to the gods. 'Just let Icarus live,' he begged. 'I''ll never ask you for anything else.' *20*

At last he felt sand and stones under his feet. He stood up and carried his son towards the shore. Icarus was still and cold. Daedalus breathed into the boy's mouth. He moved the stiff little arms up and down. Icarus was dead. *25*

## *The Icarian Sea*

With a heavy heart Daedalus buried the boy. He

*surface*, the outside of anything, in this case the top of the water.

knelt there and prayed. As he prayed he heard a bird calling above his head. He looked up and saw a small brown bird.

5 'Perdix! Remember Perdix!' the bird seemed to say. Daedalus remembered his poor young nephew. 'So this is my punishment for my crime,' he said to himself. 'Well, I deserved it.'

For a long time after that, the island was called Icarus. The sea where the boy drowned was called
10 the Icarian Sea.

# 6
## Pluto and Proserpine

Long ago, all the seasons were the same. It was never really cold and the leaves never fell from the trees. The whole earth was fresh and green all the year. The goddess Ceres took care of the crops. She was tall and golden like the corn. She was warm and kind as summer and the farmers loved her. They prayed to her before they planted their seeds. Ceres rewarded them with two or even three good harvests every year. There was peace and plenty everywhere.

Ceres had a daughter called Proserpine. If Ceres was like the summer, Proserpine was like the spring. Her cheeks were pink and white like the flowers on the fruit trees. Her eyes were as blue as April skies. Her laugh was like clear, cold streams. Everyone loved her.

Proserpine spent the long, sunny days in the fields. Sometimes she helped her mother. Sometimes she sang and danced with the young nymphs.

Deep down under the earth the dark god, Pluto, lived. He ruled the kingdom of the dead. He had no one to share his dark home with him. He tried to find a goddess or nymph to live with him. He offered gold and jewels, but no one accepted. No one wanted to leave the sunshine behind. So Pluto became lonelier and lonelier. He thought about his life and how he could change it.

Sometimes the sound of Proserpine's songs and laughter reached Pluto in his dark palace. They made him sadder and lonelier than ever.

## The dark chariot*

At last he could bear it no longer. He fastened his horses to his dark chariot. He shook the reins*.

'Up!' he ordered. The four great black horses raced towards the surface of the earth.

5    Proserpine was playing with a group of nymphs. They had flowers in their hands, and they were chasing her. They threw flowers at her, and she pretended to cry and run away. It was rather a silly game, but they were all enjoying it very much.

10  Proserpine was helpless with laughter. Her cheeks were pink and her eyes shone. Suddenly the ground shook. A hole opened at her feet. Smoke and steam came out of the hole. Proserpine heard the thunder of horses' hoofs. With a crash of thunder Pluto's

15  dark chariot appeared.

The laughter died on her lips. The nymphs picked up their skirts and ran. Proserpine turned to run too but Pluto reached out and caught her arm.

'Not so fast, my pretty one,' he said. He looked at

20  her beautiful, frightened face and his heart was filled with love. 'You shall be my queen,' he said. 'I will give you all my gold and jewels. You shall rule the land of the dead with me.'

## Pluto drives away

As he spoke Pluto felt very sad. He realized that

25  Proserpine would never agree to go with him. He had to *make* her go. He held her arm more tightly.

*chariot*, a vehicle pulled by horses. *reins*, narrow pieces of leather used to guide horses.

50

The nymphs ran away, screaming with fear. They hid in the woods and streams. Pluto picked Proserpine up in his arms and lifted her into the chariot. He had to get away at once. He did not want Ceres to see him. He shook the reins and shouted to his horses. The chariot flew along. Proserpine shut her eyes and held onto the sides of the chariot.

Pluto reached a river. He got ready to drive his horses through the water. But the nymph of the river saw Proserpine. She made the river water rise up. Great waves appeared and Pluto's horses were afraid. Pluto realized they could not go that way. But he could not turn back either; there was no time to lose. He shouted, 'Open!' and pointed at the ground. At once a great hole opened in front of him. Horses and chariot dived down into the darkness. Pluto was returning to his kingdom.

*The lost belt*

Proserpine saw the nymph of the river. She knew the nymph was trying to save her. 'Tell my mother!' Proserpine cried. She took off her belt and threw it into the water.

Pluto put his big hand over Proserpine's mouth. 'Quiet!' he ordered. The ground closed again over their heads.

That evening Ceres came home. Proserpine usually ran to greet her. This time, however, everything was quiet.

'She's hiding somewhere,' thought Ceres. 'She will jump out in a moment, and surprise me.'

'I'm coming to find you!' she called aloud. There was no answer. Ceres looked all over the house. It was empty. Then Ceres became worried. She lit a torch and went out to look for her daughter. She
5 looked for her all night and when morning came, there was still no sign of Proserpine.

Ceres forgot her duties. She did not listen to the prayers of the people. She spent every minute of every day looking for her lost child. The crops failed.
10 The ground was dry and dead. The leaves fell from the trees. People all over the world were dying of hunger.

### The nymph speaks

The people prayed to Ceres. They begged her to be their friend again. 'We need you!' they said. 'Come
15 back to us and make our fields green again.'

Ceres heard their prayers, but she shook her head sadly. She could not think of anything except her lost daughter.

A few days later, however, she was standing sadly
20 by a river when a little wave rose up. It touched her foot. She looked down and saw a belt at her feet.

'Thank you,' breathed Ceres. She picked up the belt. It was her daughter's belt; she was sure of that. She looked at it with tears in her eyes.
25 Then a fountain came up out of the ground in front of her. The sound of the water seemed to Ceres like a voice. She listened carefully, and heard the words, 'I am the nymph of the fountain. I have come up from the centre of the earth. Great Ceres, I have
30 seen your daughter. She was sitting on a golden

chair beside King Pluto. She was wearing many jewels but her cheeks were thin and white and her eyes were sad. Save her, Ceres, or she will die.'


## Ceres goes to Jupiter

Ceres thanked the nymph. She hurried to Mount Olympus and asked to speak to Jupiter. He was the     5
father of all the gods. He was wise and fair. Ceres was sure he would help her.

'I know where my daughter is,' she told him. 'She is a prisoner of the god Pluto in the kingdom of the dead. Please order Pluto to give her back to me.     10
Then the earth will be green again and my people will be happy.'

Jupiter sat and thought for a moment. 'Has she eaten anything in Pluto's kingdom?' he asked. 'If she has, she belongs to him. If she has not, I shall be     15
able to save her.'

Jupiter sent for Pluto. The dark god appeared in a cloud of smoke. 'Please bring Proserpine to me,' Jupiter ordered.

'I won't,' said Pluto.     20

Jupiter gave him an angry look.

'Get her, before I strike you!' he roared. Pluto knew all about Jupiter's lightning. He went to fetch Proserpine.

Ceres cried when she saw how thin and sad her     25
daughter looked. She held her hand in front of her eyes. The light hurt her. Ceres ran to greet her, but Jupiter stopped her.

'Not yet,' he said. He turned to Proserpine. 'Dear child,' he said, 'I want to return you to your mother.     30

But I must be fair to Pluto too. Tell me, did you eat anything — anything at all — while you were in the kingdom of the dead?'

## The apple

Proserpine's eyes filled with tears. 'He offered me
5   many things,' she said. 'He put wonderful feasts on golden dishes, and I refused everything. At last he brought a lovely red apple from my mother's own tree. I ate half of it. Look!' She held up a half-eaten apple. Ceres gave a cry of pain.
10   'She is mine!' roared Pluto.

'No!' begged Ceres. 'Please, Jupiter, help us.'

'Listen, both of you,' said Jupiter. 'I must be fair to you both; now hear my answer. Proserpine must spend half of every year with Pluto. The other half
15   of the year, she may return to the surface. Proserpine, you may now spend six months with your mother. Pluto, come back in six months' time.'

Ceres kissed Jupiter's feet. Then she took her daughter in her arms. 'Come home, dear,' she said.
20   Pluto looked hard at them. 'My time will come,' he said with a bitter laugh. He jumped into his dark chariot and drove away.

And so winter came to the earth. Every year, after the harvest, Proserpine said goodbye to her mother
25   and all her friends. She spent six months in the kingdom of the dead. Then the leaves fell from the trees. Nothing would grow in the fields and the earth fell asleep. In spring, however, Proserpine came back. The earth woke from its winter sleep the
30   trees turned green and everyone was glad.

# 7
# *A Wonderful Musician**

Orpheus lived in Greece a long time ago. He was a
most wonderful musician. When he played his lyre
the birds stopped singing. They stood in a circle
around him and listened to his beautiful music.
When he sang the nymphs and satyrs came out of 5
the woods. They gathered round · Orpheus and
begged him to continue. Orpheus's music made
everyone forget their sad, bitter and wicked
thoughts. It made everyone feel happy and good.

Orpheus had a wife called Eurydice. He loved her 10
very much. He made up many of his best songs for
her. She was fresh and young and lovely, and they
made each other very happy.

One day Eurydice was out in the fields picking
flowers with several other girls. Eurydice wanted to 15
put the flowers in the bedroom to surprise her
husband. Suddenly a snake crawled out from under
a bush. Before Eurydice could move away, its
poisonous teeth bit her foot. She gave a little cry
and fell to the ground. Her companions rushed to 20
help her. They carried her home to Orpheus.

*Eurydice dies*

Orpheus did everything he could for her but the
poison was already in her blood. In a few hours she

*musician*, someone who plays music and is good at it.

55

was dead. Orpheus's sadness was terrible to see. He picked up his lyre and tried to play. The music was so low and sad that even the rocks and the trees began to cry. He tried to sing, but he could not. The nymphs and satyrs were sad too. They loved Eurydice and they were sorry for Orpheus.

At last he could not bear his lonely life any longer. He decided to go and look for her in the kingdom of the dead. This was a terrible, dangerous thing to do.

'If I succeed, we shall be together in life,' he said. 'If I fail, then I shall die. Pluto will take me to her, and we shall be together in death. I must go now; I cannot live without her.'

He went to the river of death. There the dark boatman waited. His job was to take the spirits* of the dead people across the river into the dark kingdom.

'Boatman!' called Orpheus. 'I am looking for my wife. Will you take me across the river?'

'This ferry is for the spirits of the dead,' the boat-man replied. 'I cannot take *you*.'

Orpheus made no answer. He picked up his lyre and began to play. He sang a long, sweet, sad song.

The boatman listened. His cold, hard heart seemed to melt. Tears ran down his cheeks. 'I will take you but it is a dangerous place,' he said.

## The terrible dog

They reached the far bank of the river of death. Orpheus climbed out and looked around him. He

---

* *spirits*, those parts of people which continue to live after the body has died.

was at the gate of the dark kingdom. There stood a fierce, terrible dog. It was as big as a horse, and it had three heads. Each head had a pair of fire-red eyes and a large number of sharp yellow teeth.

5 The dog saw Orpheus and began to show all its teeth. It was ready to attack Orpheus and tear him apart. However, Orpheus picked up his lyre and began to play. The music was soft and gentle. The dog lay down on its back and waved its legs in the

10 air. Orpheus scratched the dog under all three hairy chins. It shut its six eyes and licked his fingers with its three big pink tongues.

'You're a nice old dog,' said Orpheus. 'You'll let me go through the gate, won't you?' The dog waved

15 its tail and licked Orpheus again. With shaking hands the musician opened the gate. A dark, twisting path led to the palace of the dark god. Orpheus followed it for many miles.

### The dark god

At last Orpheus came into an open space. In front

20 of him was a palace. The great doors were open wide. Orpheus marched in and found himself in a wide hall. There sat Pluto with his young wife, Proserpine, at his side.

'What are you doing here?' roared Pluto when he

25 saw Orpheus. 'No living man enters my halls. There must be some mistake. Who sent you here? Tell me, and I will punish him.'

'There is no mistake,' said Orpheus. 'I came here to look for my wife, Eurydice. A snake bit her and

30 she died. It was only a few days ago but it seems

like years. Great Pluto, I cannot live without her. Let me take her home with me now.'

Pluto looked at Proserpine and whispered something. The young goddess whispered something back. She seemed to want her husband to grant  *5*  Orpheus's wish but the dark god shook his head.

Then Orpheus touched the strings of his lyre. He sang about his love for Eurydice. He sang about her cruel, sudden death. He sang about his lonely life since then. The god's dark eyes became bright with  *10*  tears. Proserpine hid her lovely face in her hands and cried. The spirits of the dead gathered round to listen, and they cried too.

*Pluto grants Orpheus's prayer*

When Orpheus had finished, Pluto spoke. 'Very well,' he said, 'I will grant your prayer. You can take  *15*  your wife home now.' He called to two of the spirits. 'Bring Eurydice here.' Orpheus went down on his knees and kissed the dark god's feet. Pluto raised his hand.

'Wait,' he said. 'Just one thing. You must not look  *20*  back at your wife until you have passed through my gates. If you look back, she will be lost for ever.'

'Oh, thank you!' cried Orpheus. 'I promise.'

They brought Eurydice to him. She was very thin and grey like a shadow but she knew him, and she  *25*  smiled and held out her hands to him. Proserpine kissed her goodbye. Then Orpheus and Eurydice began their dangerous journey.

They went along the dark twisting path. Orpheus could see the gates a few steps in front of him. But  *30* was Eurydice still following him? He could not be sure.

'Just one look,' he thought. 'Pluto will never know. I can't go through the gates without her!' He
5  turned his head and gave one quick look. Eurydice was only a few steps behind. As soon as he looked, she stopped. She put out her arms to him. She opened her mouth to speak, but no sound came out.

'Eurydice, follow me!' cried Orpheus. 'We are
10  almost there. Only a few more steps.'

Very sadly she shook her head. Her shadow became thinner and greyer; then she disappeared.


## Orpheus returns to Earth

Orpheus went out through the gate. The terrible dog licked his hand and wanted to play. Orpheus
15  cried on its great hairy shoulder. He went to the river and asked the boatman to help him. When he had told his story, the boatman just shook his head.

'You had your chance,' he said. 'Pluto will never grant your prayer a second time. Go home, young
20  man, and try to forget the past.'

For seven days and nights Orpheus sat by the river without food or sleep. At last he returned to the green earth. He went up onto a high mountain. He lived a sad, lonely life there. He lived with the
25  birds, the trees and the wild animals. If he could not have Eurydice, he did not want any other human companions.

He still played and sang. Musicians are like birds; they cannot stop singing, even when they are sad. But his songs were all sad songs.

## *The dancing women*

One day, however, Orpheus was walking on the mountain when he met a group of women. They were all singing and dancing. When they saw his lyre, they shouted to him.

'Hello! Come and play us a song!' Orpheus shook his head.

'Come on. Let's have something cheerful!' they shouted. Their voices were loud and rough and their breath smelt of wine. Orpheus tried to explain, but they would not listen.

At last the women became angry. They threw stones at him. One of them hit Orpheus on the side of the head. He fell to the ground. The women laughed and shouted and they threw more and more stones. At last he lay dying with his lyre beside him.

They threw the musician's body into the river. He floated down the river, and his last words were, 'Eurydice! Eurydice!'

Everything — the trees, the birds, the animals, even the rocks — felt sad. The wood nymphs and water nymphs forgot their games and cried for the sweet singer.

They were wrong to be sad. Orpheus crossed the river of death with a light heart. The boatman welcomed him and took him across the river. The fierce three-headed dog licked his hand to greet him. At the entrance stood Eurydice. He rushed forward to meet his dear wife. She threw her arms around his neck. Orpheus and Eurydice were together again, and nothing could separate them.

# Questions

## 1
### The First Spider

A. How was Minerva born?
B. Why was she jealous of Arachne?
C. Why are spiders called Arachnidae?
D. How did Minerva dress before she visited Arachne?

## 2
### The Golden Touch

A. Who was Dionysus, and who was Silenus?
B. Why did Dionysns say he would grant King Midas a wish?
C. When did Midas first realize that his golden touch could bring trouble?
D. Imagine that someone has granted you one wish. What will you wish for?
E. What do you think this story is trying to tell us?

## 3
### The Donkey's Ears

A. Why was there a contest and who was tho judge?
B. What was Pan's music like? How did the audience feel when they heard it?
C. What happened when Midas woke next morning?

D. How did he hide the donkey's ears?

# 4
## Theseus and the Minotaur

A. What was unusual about King Minos's pet, and where did it live?
B. Why did Aegeus leave his wife and child?
C. Why did Minos's son want to go to Athens?
D. How did the people choose the unlucky fourteen?

# 5
## The Wonderful Wings

A. Why did Daedalus and Icarus run away from Athens?
B. How did they escape from Crete?
C. Why did Icarus crash into the sea?
D. Where did Daedalus bury his son?

# 6
## Pluto and Proserpine

A. Why did no one want to live with Pluto?
B. Who saw Pluto taking Proserpine away, and how did that person tell Ceres?
C. How did Ceres plan to get her daughter back?
D. Why did Proserpine have to spend half of every year under the ground?

# 7
## A Wonderful Musiciam

A. Explain how Eurydice died.

B. How did Orpheus try to get her back? What went wrong?
C. Why was Orpheus's meeting with the dancing women a lucky meeting? Explain.

# Oxford Progressive English Readers

## Introductory Grade

Vocabulary restricted to 1400 headwords
Illustrated in full colour

## Grade 1

Vocabulary restricted to 2100 headwords
Illustrated in full colour

## Grade 2

Vocabulary restricted to 3100 headwords
Illustrated in colour

## Grade 2 (cont.)

| | |
|---|---|
| The Hound of the Baskervilles | Sir Arthur Conan Doyle |
| The Missing Scientist | S.F. Stevens |
| The Red Badge of Courage | Stephen Crane |
| Robinson Crusoe | Daniel Defoe |
| Seven Chinese Stories | T.J. Sheridan |
| Stories of Shakespeare's Plays 2 | Retold by Wyatt & Fullerton |
| A Tale of Two Cities | Charles Dickens |
| Tales of Crime and Detection | Retold by G.F. Wear |
| Two Boxes of Gold and Other Stories | Charles Dickens |

## Grade 3

Vocabulary restricted to 3700 headwords
Illustrated in colour

| | |
|---|---|
| Battle of Wits at Crimson Cliff | Retold by Benjamin Chia |
| Dr Jekyll and Mr Hyde and Other Stories | R.L. Stevenson |
| From Russia, with Love | Ian Fleming |
| The Gifts and Other Stories | O. Henry & Others |
| The Good Earth | Pearl S. Buck |
| Journey to the Centre of the Earth | Jules Verne |
| Kidnapped | R.L. Stevenson |
| King Solomon's Mines | H. Rider Haggard |
| Lady Precious Stream | S.I. Hsiung |
| The Light of Day | Eric Ambler |
| Moonraker | Ian Fleming |
| The Moonstone | Wilkie Collins |
| A Night of Terror and Other Strange Tales | Guy De Maupassant |
| Seven Stories | H.G. Wells |
| Stories of Shakespeare's Plays 3 | Retold by H.G. Wyatt |
| Tales of Mystery and Imagination | Edgar Allan Poe |
| 20,000 Leagues Under the Sea | Jules Verne |
| The War of the Worlds | H.G. Wells |
| The Woman in White | Wilkie Collins |
| Wuthering Heights | Emily Brontë |
| You Only Live Twice | Ian Fleming |

## Grade 4

Vocabulary within a 5000 headwords range
Illustrated in black and white

| | |
|---|---|
| The Diamond as Big as the Ritz and Other Stories | F. Scott Fitzgerald |
| Dragon Seed | Pearl S. Buck |
| Frankenstein | Mary Shelley |
| The Mayor of Casterbridge | Thomas Hardy |
| Pride and Prejudice | Jane Austen |
| The Stalled Ox and Other Stories | Saki |
| The Thimble and Other Stories | D.H. Lawrence |